BOTH SIDES OF THE CATFLAP

poems by
Sandy Brownjohn

illustrations by Liz Pichon

Hodder
Children's
Books

a division of Hodder Headline plc

Dedicated to the memory of
Leslie and Margaret Willingham

Bucket and Spade and *Footprints* first appeared in the
This Way That Way series published by
Mary Glasgow Publications 1989.

Nine Lives, Public Speaking, Growing Up,
The Fall-Out, and extracts from *A Norfolk Haiku Bestiary*
first appeared in **Poetry Express**
published by Ginn 1993

CONTENTS

My Cat and Mouse 8
Public Speaking 10
The Song of the Wild Geese 12
The Fall-Out 13
Where Have All The Flowers Gone? 14
Bucket and Spade .15
Upon Thy Belly 18
Dog Met Frog 20
Growing Up 21
Crushed 22
Rufus Lupin Chester 24
Umbrage (1) 26
Kennings Cat 27
A Traveller's Tale 28
The Games Lesson 30
Owl 32
Scrumping Rhyme 34
Thisbe 35
More Umbrage 38
A Norfolk Haiku Bestiary 39
Dorcas 46

Voices of the Night 48
My Bike 50
Footprints 53
Eenymeenyminymice 54
The Ship of State 55
Nine Lives 56
Owl in the Afternoon 58
The White Highlands of England 60
Bottled Up 63
No Earthly Reason .66
Shall We Walk? 68
Childhood 70
From a Sick Bed 71
He May Be Some Time 72
Christmas Eve 74
Dunwich to Sizewell: Suffolk 78
Blackmail 80
Snails of a Summer Night 82
Dinner Time 84
David and Goliath .87

MY CAT AND MOUSE

There's a crisis and commotion at the catflap,
A kerfuffle of a scuffle in the hall,
A contretemps of shattering proportions,
A scowling and a yowling caterwaul.

For framed in the window of the catflap
A no-hoper interloper to the house
Is punching at the perspex with his southpaw –
It's the mighty muscled moggy called Mouse.

And flat-eared on the inside of the catflap,
Defender of her gender and her patch,
Her fluffed-up body puffed-up to look larger,
Stands Dorcas with her claws all poised to scratch.

There's a spitting and a hitting at the catflap,
Then a deep-throated rumble of a growl.
From a grumble to a strangle of a gurgle
It erupts in an eerie hollow howl.

Now this happens every day at the catflap
And in vain I explain she'll always win,
For though there are two sides to every catflap
This one's locked and *he can't come in.*

PUBLIC SPEAKING

When cows inquire "How do you do?",
   They moo.

When horses give you the time of day,
   They neigh.

When dogs pass the odd remark,
   They bark.

When ducks need to answer back,
   They quack.

When cats wholeheartedly concur,
   They purr.

When pigs are moved to file a report,
   They snort.

When owls are asked to make a speech,
   They screech.

When sheep are forced to think on their feet,
    They bleat.

But when I'm called upon to speak,
    I squeak.

I mumble and mutter,
I stumble and stutter,
And tie my tongue into a knot.

What have they got
That I have not?

THE SONG OF THE WILD GEESE

We're wild winter geese and we gather together
With other goose brothers, whatever the weather.
A blether of nagging, we gabble and babble,
A gaggle of trouble, they call us a rabble.

Gregarious feeding's a great greedy squabble
And various seedlings we grub up and gobble.
They call us ungainly and robbers who plunder,
But watch us take off in a crowd and then wonder:

Like waves in dream water we fly in formations
And furrow the sky with our fluid quotations
Like long lines of handwriting sprawled on the paper.
They waft on the wind-drift like trails of vapour.

And what are these phrases our wingbeats are telling,
What secrets wrapped up in the words we are spelling?
Well -
If you have forgotten what needn't be said,
The days of your reading such stories are dead.

THE FALL-OUT

A quarrel is a pair of scissors
Scoring points that go too deep,
And with steel in their cold hearts
Two people cut each other to shreds.

WHERE HAVE ALL THE FLOWERS GONE?

When I was ten and sometimes good
Bluebells grew in Whomerley Wood,
But I pulled at them till they squeaked in pain
Not knowing they wouldn't grow again.

My sister and I picked them all
And sold them in bunches from a stall
At sixpence each, and people came
Till mother dragged us home in shame.

"Just what do you think you're doing," she said,
"No better than beggars." We were sent to bed.
The rest of the bluebells were given away,
And none grow in the wood today.

BUCKET AND SPADE

Down among the rockpools,
Underneath the cliff,
On a beach in Anglia
Where the wind is stiff,
Children all are moaning,
"Take us to the Fair",
While dads are a-digging,
Building castles in the air.

Herring gulls are nesting
High up in the chalk,
Laughing at the people
In their low-pitched squawk.
"Mum, it's really boring!
More fun at the Fair."
But dad goes on a-digging
His great castle in the air.

"Take interest in the wildlife,
There's shrimps in all those pools.
Forget about the slot machines,
They're only made for fools.
And *do* stop whining,
You're worse than him out there.
Go and help your father
Build his castle in the air."

If I could have my spade back
I'd build one of my own,
With turrets, dungeons, battlements,
A drawbridge made of stone;
Shells for decoration,
A moat to circle round,
And a flag to crown in glory
My castle on the ground.

But dad won't let me near his,
Says he's building it for me.
I have to take the bucket
To fetch water from the sea.
Millions of trips. But then
He pours it in with care.
As if I'd *want* to trample on
His castle in the air.

UPON THY BELLY

(*'Upon thy belly shalt thou go, and dust shalt thou eat all the days of thy life.' - Genesis 3, 14*)

Tread lightly through the bracken,
Thread softly through the air,
Lift each foot with caution,
Put it down with care,
Keep your eyes open
And your ears alert
For the zigzag viper,
The V-sign zigzag viper,
The unsung, tonguing viper
Snaking through the dirt.

Crash boldly through the undergrowth,
Dash madly through the fern,
Break the sonic barrier
So the snake will learn
To hide away from you
Because he is afraid,
The zigzag patterned viper,
The shy zigzag viper,
The hissing, missing viper
Slithering into shade.

DOG MET FROG

One hoppy frog, a water-lily topper
One soppy dog, a sunshine flopper

Frog hops up with a plolloppy lolloppy
Hops in the pond with a flip-flopper plop

Dog pops up with a flolloppy slolloppy
Drops in the pond with a belly-flopper slop

Dog comes a cropper it's a whopper of a drop

What a hip-hoppy frog!
What a tip-toppy frog!
What a slip-sloppy dog!
What a drip-droppy dog!

Dog met frog.   One wet dog.

GROWING UP

Once she was carefree
And played with her toys,
She lived in her own world
And didn't like boys.

Now she works hard
And plays with her friends.
As to liking the boys –
Well, it rather depends...

CRUSHED

Out on the edge, where the playground meets the grassland,
A little girl is sitting and crying alone.
Over the playground the pigeons are winging
But she doesn't see them, her eyes are still stinging
With tears at the insults the others were slinging
To force her to go off and play on her own.

A little girl is sitting and crying her eyes out,
Surrounded by sharp sticks and pointed stones.
High up above her the skylarks are singing
But she doesn't hear them, her ears are still ringing
With all the untruths the others were flinging.
– And these are the words they say cannot break bones.

RUFUS LUPIN CHESTER

Rufus Lupin Chester
Has a name with which to conjure
But it wasn't always so,
No, it wasn't always so.

Abandoned as a kitten
He just roamed the lanes of Catton
For he had nowhere to go,
No, he had nowhere to go,

Till a kind cat-loving stranger
Took a shine to little 'ginger'.
Scooping up the harum-scarum,
She delivered him to Dereham
To the League for Cats' Protection,
Whence, to his great satisfaction,
He has found a doting owner.
And he's really on a winner,
For this rescued cat of courage
Now has pride of place at Norwich

Where he's living with my sister.
Yes, with Rufus Lupin Chester
You would never ever know
That it wasn't always so.

UMBRAGE (1)

Somebody's pinched my umbrella, the swine!
There ought to be an enormous fine.
If I knew who it was I could probably sue,
Or, better still, set a penance to do
Which involved standing out in the pouring rain
Against the might of a hurricane
Without any place to shelter in
So they were soaked right through to the skin
And had to watch the deluge descend
For hours and hours and hours on end.

KENNINGS CAT

Tail–**flicker**
Fur–**licker**
Tree–**scratcher**
Mouse–**catcher**
Basket–**sleeper**
Night–**creeper**
Eye–**blinker**
Milk–**drinker**
Lap–**sitter**
Ball–**hitter**
Fish–**eater**
Fire–**heater**
String–**muddler**
Kitten–**cuddler**
Angry–**hisser**
Wet–**kisser**
Wall–**prowler**
Moon–**howler**
Cream–**lapper**
Claw–**tapper**
Cat–**flapper**

A TRAVELLER'S TALE

A ship sailed into harbour
And golden were its sails,
Its deck was silver and the crew
Told strange inviting tales.

They called to me to join them,
Believe in us, they said,
And we will show you how to weave
The stories in your head.

From myths of northern forests
And eastern mysteries
To where the sun sets in the west
And dreams of southern seas,

From voices in the shadows
And whispers in the dark
To cries that echo round the skies
And words that leave their mark,

From deeps of coral oceans
To hills of starry cloud,
From eyes that glimmer in the night
To sockets through a shroud,

From hopes of life eternal
To fears of the unknown,
From where an X will mark the spot
And magic carves the stone,

Our ship is heavy laden.
The cargo in our hold
Is precious beyond all your dreams
And can't be bought or sold.

So why not come and join us,
This chance will be withdrawn,
Our ship won't pass this way again,
We sail with the dawn.

THE GAMES LESSON

The field was large, and round the edge
Were bushes, trees and long grass where
Imagination stirred.

Miss Evans said, "Now find a space
Away from anybody else."
We took her at her word.

In all directions we dispersed
To find our space and be alone
Where distances were blurred.

Miss Evans, helpless, watched us go
And called to us, "Come back at once,
This really is absurd."

But we were far away by then
And learning from the outside world
Where her voice was not heard.

And hundreds of Miss Evanses
Still peer shortsighted after us,
Uncertain what occurred.

OWL

```
                              S
                            S H
                          S H H
        O W L             S H H
      P R O W L S     L O W
      S H O W S     S L O W
        L O W   L O O P
          S W O O S H
          S W O O P S
          W H O O P S
        W O O O
      W O O O
    W O O
      W
  O O
  O O
```

SCRUMPING RHYME

Scrumper, scrumper,
Stick 'em up your jumper,

If the farmer catches you
He's likely to thump yer.
Apples in the orchard
Lying on the grass,
Jump off the wall and
Land on your
Feet step quietly,
All keep 'mum',
The farmer has a big stick
To hit you on the
Way back to the gate,
Over you come,
Stolen apples taste good
But upset the
Scrumper, scrumper,
Stick 'em up your jumper,

If the farmer catches you
He's likely to thump yer.

THISBE

My cat's a Manx cat,
She cannot chase her tail,
Though every night
With all her might
She tries so hard.
It's such a sight
To see her racing
Round our flat,
In through this door,
Out through that,
As if the wind
Were in her tail,
But all to no avail
Because
My cat's a Manx cat,
She has no tail.

My cat's a Rumpy
From Douglas, Isle of Man.
In days of old
The Vikings bold
Killed for tails,
Or so we're told,
To plume their helmets.
So into the dales
The mother cats went,
Bit off the tails
Of new-born cats
So they weren't slain.
Now comes by boat and train
To me
My tabby Rumpy
From the Isle of Man.

My cat's a Manx cat,
And thereby hangs a tale,
For some say
That far away
And long ago
It made its way
To Noah's Ark
But was the last.
Its tail was caught
When the door shut fast.
So, tailless cats
Came two by two.
I believe it, don't you?
For
My cat's a Manx cat.
This is her tale.

MORE UMBRAGE

A curse on those who take umbrellas!
May every spoke unhinge, as well as
Bend and break, stick at an angle
Resisting attempts to disentangle.
May strong winds buffet the brollies about
And blow them irrevocably inside-out.
Stolen umbrellas of the world unite!
Put up a once-and-for-all last fight
To punish those who are so fell as
To pilfer other people's umbrellas.

A NORFOLK HAIKU BESTIARY

a
Ants in straggly lines,
Marching over pavement cracks,
Stop to wave at friends.

b
A tiny flitter
Through the dusk – watch the shy bat
Inhabit his world.

c
Cat – King of the Beasts.
Even a common moggy
Has the regal air.

d
A dragonfly darts
Here, there, across the wooden
Path on the marshes.

e Eels slip from your hands
Like long, fat, black spaghetti
Down the river's plug.

f Caught in Spring sunlight,
The finch pecks at the blossom.
No apples this year.

g Before each foot falls
Grasshoppers fountain into
Air like lawn sprinklers.

h A hedgehog stands up
So much further off the ground
And she outruns you.

i

Spindly ichneumon,
With flimsy wings by night light,
Whiskers up the wall.

j

Two jays mob the cat.
Their jabber clatters at each
Scratchy ratchet screech.

k

In wrapt suspension
A kestrel ignores the cars.
He knows about speed.

l

The little black lamb
In a field of all-white sheep
Loves the attention.

m
Under the front lawn
A mole, with his strong shoulders,
Makes many mountains.

n
Natterjacks crossing
Syderstone Road take their lives
In their clammy hands.

o
Owl haunts like a wraith
While the hedgerow holds its breath.
Death is on the wing.

p
Peacock butterfly
Lands on lilac in bright sun.
See, she blinks her eyes.

q
The queen of the hive
Cannot fly free; she mothers
A whole dynasty.

r
A rat on the beam
Of the barn shows just how large
His presence can be.

s
Along the field's edge
Undulates a slender stoat
Like a small ripple.

t
The slow old tortoise
Cranes his leathery neck and
Wrinkled folds uncrease.

U

Cream-white skeletons
Of urchins adorn the shore
Like empty lockets.

V

A vole's limp body
Droops from the cat's mouth – one more
Unwelcome present.

Like sharks of the air
Wasps nosily cruise about.
Beware! They backbite.

Christmas at Holkham:
One crossbill hides from twitchers
Who all look alike.

Y Tillip! Tillip! Tjip!
The yellowhammer chitters,
And strictly no – cheese!

Z Lie low, Fenland fish.
The zander's fanged jaws have an
Appetite to kill.

DORCAS

Ho, there! Fish-face,
Is that nice and warm?
Lying on the window sill
Soaking your sleek and shining fill,
Letting the August hot sun spill
On to your stretched out form,
That is your morning place.

Ho, there! Fur-ball,
Twitching in your sleep.
Body curled up on the bed,
Paws tucked over round your head,
Not a flicker at my tread,
Nor even slant-eyed peep
Till night begins to fall.

Ho, there! Wide-eyes,
Whiskers to the fore.
Ears alert as darkness grows,
Belly low and pointing nose,
Woe betide tonight all those
Who fear red tooth and claw
And would not be your prize.

VOICES OF THE NIGHT

We are the shadows that creep in the night
And hide in the corners behind your bed,
And after you've turned out the comforting light
We burrow into your sleepy head.

We are the sounds of the silent room,
The clock with its ominous regular ticks,
The creaks as the floorboards contract in the gloom,
The doorhandle's sudden unsettling clicks.

We are the searchlights of passing cars
That swivel and sweep through the curtain's crack,
We are the glow from the luminous stars
That trace on your ceiling a zodiac.

We are the forms of familiar things
That take on a life of their own after dark,
The shadowy mobile grows threatening wings
And under the bed swims a silent shark.

We are each knob and handle and hook
Transformed into faces and frightening shapes.
The walls huddle round and wherever you look
A black void in the bedroom gapes.

MY BIKE

My bike is my trusty steed,
Fit for a shining knight indeed.
He'll prance and advance
As I charge with my lance,
His hooves beat out thunder,
The crowd roars in wonder,
But all I can hear
Is the wind in my ear.
Fair maidens hold their breath
For this tournament with death.
But I gallop straight and my aim is true;
The black knight is down, I have run him through.
The cheers echo around the ground
As, I the victor, kneel to be crowned.

Today my bike is a pirate ship
Tacking the road on her ocean trip.
We slide and glide
Through the countryside,
On the seven seas
We board who we please;
Be they French or Spanish
Their treasure will vanish
And they'll go to their watery graves
Beneath the grey tarmac waves.
I'm captain and lookout and all of the crew,
The wind's in the rigging, you'd better heave to,
For I am a Sea-Wolf, I'm bold and I'm free!
– At least, I am till it's time for tea.

My bike's a bucking bronco,
Scourge of the wild west rodeo.
It brakes and jumps
And shakes and bumps,
It dips and curves
And trips and swerves.
It's a show of a tussle
For a rider with muscle
And the spectators cheer to a fault
Till it skids to an untimely halt.
The bike for a moment's suspended in air,
And so am I with my devil-may-care,
But it's over the handlebars now that I must
And another cowboy bites the dust.

FOOTPRINTS

Wherever I go my footprints will follow
Leaving a trail that knows its own way.

Walk on water, head held high,
My footprints will follow me, wet or dry.

Wherever I go it will be to advance,
My footprint partners will join the dance.

Follow in my footprints if you will,
I'll lead you on, I'll never stand still.

If the ground is soft or the ground is hard
You won't catch my footprints off their guard.

Wherever I go I will leave my mark.
My footprints will follow me into the dark.

EENYMEENYMINY MICE

Eenymeenyminy Mice	hobnob on a picnic
Abracadabra	razzamatazz
Roly–poly	higgledy–piggledy
Helter–skelter	pell–mell
Harum–scarum	willy–nilly
Jelly–belly	silly–billy
Airy–fairy	fuddy–duddy
Hocus–pocus	hanky–panky
Walkie–talkie	pow–wow
Hugger–mugger	hotch–potch
Super–duper	pooper–scooper

THE SHIP OF STATE

The baker, the thatcher, the major and the clerk,
Set to sea in a leaky barque.
"Ho!" said the baker, "Well, this is a lark!"
But he fell overboard and was lost in the dark.

The thatcher, the major, and the clerk looked round,
And each one feared he would soon be drowned.
"Ho!" said the thatcher, "I'll swim to dry ground,"
Then sank in a freak wave and never was found.

The major and the clerk both thought they should check
Just how much water was on the deck.
"Ho!" said the major, "It's up to my neck!
If we don't row fast then the ship will wreck!"

The major and the clerk then knew it was a race
To reach the shore, so they kept up the pace.
"Ho!" said the clerk, "We'll sink without trace!"
But – the clerk washed up with a smile on his face.

NINE LIVES

i.m. Thisbe (1976-1990)

This is my grave by the holly tree,
Remember me?

I am the cat who arrived by rail
Without a tail.

I am the cat who tried walking on water
Which would not support her.

I am the cat who got stuck on the ledge,
Too near the edge.

I am the cat who was locked in the shed
And could not be fed.

I am the cat who ran in the road
Where traffic flowed.

I am the cat who spat in the night
And lost the fight.

I am the cat who hid out in the snow
When you wanted to go.

I am the cat who with arthritic bones
Concealed her groans.

I am the cat who that Autumn day
Just faded away.

This is my grave by the holly tree.
Remember me.

OWL IN THE AFTERNOON

On silent wings from nowhere came the owl;
How violent, yet how soft, the rush of air
That brushed my hair.

The winter sky was blue and clear and light,
But paled away to white there at the edge,
Just where the hedge

Marked out the line dividing sky from earth.
The owl swung wide, and clearly knew the place;
It flew with grace

Along the verges up and down the lane.
Such big round eyes and soundless beating prowl,
This fleeting owl;

So easy to admire it on the wing
And not to hear the squeal of its kill.
The real thrill

Was being there and seeing it survive;
For don't we all, in some way, browse with death
Each mouse's breath?

THE WHITE HIGHLANDS OF ENGLAND

(For J.B.)

In the white heat of an afternoon
My friend and I
Spent our time on a shingle beach
Under a tolerant sky.

Neither of us was aware at all,
My friend and I,
Of the white gulls, the white clouds
And the white passers-by.

We talked of what was common to both,
My friend and I,
Of life and truth, of health and death,
And what had made us cry.

We sighed and laughed all afternoon,
My friend and I,
While white foam broke on bleached stones
And left them there to dry.

In an English tearoom near the church
My friend and I
Ate white scones with country cream
Till we had to say "Goodbye".

Past white walls of cottages,
My friend and I
Had been where white net curtains can
Conceal the white lie,

But it did not even cross our minds
To have to try.
We just got on like brother and sister,
My Jamaican friend and I.

BOTTLED UP

I'm a lonely little bottle bank,
I'm told I'm one of three,
But I don't know who my mother was,
I have no family
And on this garage forecourt
There is only one of me.

And on this garage forecourt
The tyre pressure-gauge
Talks a lot of hot air
And craves centre-stage.
He teases me about my size
And puts me in a rage.

He teases me about my size,
All because I'm fat,
Says, I'm just a hollow vessel
– Well, he'd know about that! –
Though I'm green by name and nature
I'd like to squash him flat.

Though I'm green by name and nature
And I don't know much of life,
I know the world is better
If love replaces strife,
Oh, and I'm in love with a petrol pump,
I wish she'd be my wife.

Oh, I'm in love with a petrol pump,
She's beautiful and slim
And everything that I am not,
She's upright, neat and trim,
But she won't even look at me.
So life is pretty grim.

She won't even look at me,
And nor will anyone.
I'm only good for rubbish
When all is said and done.
I swallow up the broken glass
Of other people's fun.

I swallow up the broken glass,
My mouth is open wide.
My heart is full splinters,
My world is smashed inside.
I'm a lonely little bottle bank,

– But I still have my pride.

NO EARTHLY REASON

They say the way to a happier life
Is down the road old Annie took.
With her buttons done up and her stout shoes on
She packed her bags with a faraway look
And strode off into her own sunset.
Remoter than distant and wider than free
She was gone where we could not see.

They say the way to a happier life
Is the route old Mary chose to take.
With her sleeves rolled up and and her pinafore on
She slipped unnoticed into the lake.
She reached rock bottom and floated away;
Deeper than under, more down than below
She was gone where we could not know.

They say the way to a happier life
Is where old Betsy stepped content.
With her skirt tucked up and her warm coat on
She waved, then simply upped and went.
She opened her brolly and flew to the stars;
Further than upward and higher than tall
She was gone for good and all.

SHALL WE WALK?

Two fleas had hopped a ride upon a passing cat.
I fancy that,
Said one flea to his mate,
So many hot dinners – all on one plate!

A paradise for gourmets, a peripatetic delight.
Let's have a bite.
An unexpected treat,
Our very own Good Food Guide on four feet.

With so much on the menu they wondered where to start;
The À La Carte?
Perhaps the Dish of the Day?
A taste of shoulder, leg or back? They couldn't say.

But, he who hesitates, we know, is often lost,

As they found to their cost

When they finally came to sup,

For a great, rough tongue – came and licked them up.

CHILDHOOD

(For C.C.)

The key is old, its teeth are worn,
The locks have changed since we were born.
The door which opened with this key
Is overgrown, and memory
Can't find the way back through the wood,
And might not know it if it could.

This is the key to a closed door
Where each of us has been before,
But now it's hidden in the mist
Where all things go which don't exist.
This is our common tragedy –
That all we're left with is the key.

FROM A SICK BED

Spider, spin your spool for me,
Spin me a thread to swing me free.

Something's calling and I must go,
It won't wait long and I must know

What might have been. I'd like to chance
Asking the world for one more dance

Or else the shadow in shapely guise
Will weave a web to close my eyes.

Spider, then you must hide away,
And if you love life, you must pray.

HE MAY BE SOME TIME

(For Carol)

Have you seen Ubu?
He has black and white fur.
He doesn't like to fight,
Well, not any more.

Have you seen Ubu?
– Voted 'Cat of the Year'?
He's not in the colonel's shed
Or sleeping in the car.

Have you seen Ubu?
– The literary cat
Who kept a holiday diary
    when we got back?

        een Ubu?
        on your face
        ontentment

Have you seen Ubu?
He couldn't have gone far.
He just went outside, it seems,
For evermore.

CHRISTMAS EVE

Our mother was tearing her hair out,
(My sister and I played upstairs),
There was too much to do,
She would never be through,
And the air was quite blue;
So father had made himself scarce.

He'd been sent to do last-minute shopping
With a list as long as your arm.
Then to us mother said,
"You be useful instead,
Go and clear up the shed –
And leave me some peace to get calm!"

We put on our coats and our wellies
And moaned as we went through the door.
The thick cloud hung low,
And its strange, muddy glow
Held the promise of snow,
And the wind was quite biting and raw.

Our shed wasn't much of a building –
Its door had come off long ago.
What was once a tool-store
Now had cobwebs galore,
Fieldmice under the floor,
And corners where fungus could grow.

We piled things into the middle,
And on top of an old packing case
A basket was laid.
Then we propped up a spade,
Fork, and hoe as we made
A vain effort to tidy the place.

We put dirty rags in the basket,
Dragged over a bag of cement,
From a dusty wire rack
Hauled down bits of sack
And covered the back
Of each garden tool where it leant.

That evening the snow didn't happen,
The sky, full of stars, was aglow.
The moon shone its light
In the shed, and the sight
On that cold Christmas night
Made a wonder much greater than snow.

For it seemed a particular star hung
Just over the shed's wooden gable.
It silvered the floor
And the fine wisps of straw
So our old shed looked more
As if it were really a stable.

What we saw was a group of tall figures
Leaning over the cradle below.
A lamb knelt without sound,
And we looked all around
At the frost on the ground,
Hoping it might be snow.

DUNWICH TO SIZEWELL: SUFFOLK

Along this coast she rides her horse,
Pounding a wide and windswept shore,
Her foaming hair like shaggy tinsel
In the stormlight. Over inlets
Streams her flowing mane –
And no one speaks her name.

At every turning tide they leap,
This horse and woman. Faces pale
Beneath the waves and drowned bells peal
As if their ringing were a plea
For decent burial and last rites,
But this witch never tires.

Every year the high seas send
The white horse chomping at the ends
Of cliffs, homes, churches' gates,
And gravestones worn down to the stage
That, unreadable, they sink reviled
Into the sand. May God deliver

All who live near the reactor
From it, and from the sea. Creator,
If a prayer can ever mean
Anything, then say, Amen.

(This poem employs anagram rhymes.)

BLACKMAIL

When my cat feels neglected
She can be very cross.
She simply has to make the point
That she is the boss.

If I am sitting working
And push her off the page,
She takes it very personally
And slumps in silent rage,

For umbrage has been taken.
She turns her back on me
And emanates high dudgeon where
I cannot fail to see.

No matter what I say to her
She feigns deep unconcern,
Until I grovel, beg, cajole,
Imploring her to turn.

First one ear swivels slowly,
The other twists to hear,
Then gradually her face looks round,
Its hurt expression clear.

And still she will not come to me.
I have to go to her
And make humble apologies,
Encourage her to purr.

It's only then she lets me lift
And put her on my knee
Where, settled into pride of place,
She smirks contentedly.

SNAILS OF A SUMMER NIGHT

The snails are out in Belsize Park
After the summer rain,
Their cold thick jelly bodies leech
On low white walls like lumps of sleech
On some alluvial plain.

Their horns sway slowly in the air,
One touch and they retract.
As if stuck on, their tilting homes
Are balanced high like bulbous domes
To make them look hump-backed.

The street lights pick out silver trails
And shells that seem too small
To hold a snail that can emerge
In one gelatinous brown splurge
Of slimy wrinkled crawl.

They could be from another world,
These blobs the rain will sprout;
Each one a strange and dark misfit
As if the walls had cracked and split
To let their secrets out.

('Sleech' is mud deposited by a sea or river.)

DINNER-TIME

What's the time, Mr Wolf?
-Time to set out.-
We take our first tentative steps
on our own.

What's the time, Mr Wolf?
-Time to doubt.-
We cling to others so as not
to be alone.

What's the time, Mr Wolf?
-Time to take stock.-
We see the past stretching to what
we can't retrace.

What's the time, Mr Wolf?
-Time for a shock.-
We know that we are unprepared
to see your face.

What's the time, Mr Wolf?
-Time is short.-
The distance between us and you
is certain death.

What's the time, Mr Wolf?
-Time to be caught.-
All resolve has left us now.
We feel your breath.

DAVID AND GOLIATH

DAVID AND GOLIATH

David was the son of Jesse
And he came from Bethlehem,
He kept an eye on his father's sheep
And the Lord kept an eye on him.

Yes, David was the son of Jesse
And a shepherd boy was he,
He killed a lion and he killed a bear
So the sheep and the lambs could be free.

David was the youngest brother,
There was music in his soul,
There was magic in his fingertips
When he played his harp for Saul.

Now, Saul was the King of Israel
And the Lord he disobeyed,
So the Lord decided that the time had come
To send in the Philistine brigade.

And the Lord had chosen David
To set the world to right,
But a lion and a bear could not compare
With the giant that he had to fight.

The Philistines stood on the mountain top
Looking down on the valley wide,
The Israelites stood and faced them
On the mountain on the other side.
Oh, you should have heard the shouting
And you should have heard the cries,
The Israelites were terrified –
They couldn't believe their eyes.

There stood Goliath, Goliath the giant,
Huge and defiant;
Helmet of brass and coat of mail –
He couldn't fail.
There stood Goliath with spearhead of iron.
Bolder than a lion,
Larger than life and stronger than a bear.
He shouted his dare.

Goliath, he cried to the Israelites –
Send me your champion, you cowards, to fight!
Yes, Goliath, he cried – Let him fight with me,
We'll see who's the strongest, oh yes, we'll see!

The Israelites, they shook from head to toe,
They ran so fast there was nowhere left to go.
They quaked and they trembled and they turned so white,
There wasn't anyone who was prepared to fight,
There wasn't anyone who was brave enough to fight.

The Israelites had terror in their eyes,
They'd never seen a giant half that size!
They shivered and they quivered and they turned so pale,
They looked at one another and they all turned tail,
They looked at one another and together they all turned tail.

The Israelites showed fear in every gaze.
The giant stood before them forty days.
They muttered and they stuttered and they turned their back,
There wasn't anyone who would go into attack,
There wasn't anyone with the courage to attack.

When David saw that all was lost,
He fell to thinking and counting the cost.
That night he drew himself apart
And prayed to the Lord to give him heart.

When I tended the sheep You kept me safe,
Made me strong when I killed the bear,
I defended the sheep, You kept me safe
From the lion when I killed him there.
I surrender myself to Your care.
Make me strong and guide my aim,
If You lend me the courage, I declare
I will fight this giant in Your name.

So, up spoke David, that shepherd boy –
If nobody will fight him then we'll all be destroyed.
If you won't do it, it'll have to be me.
But they burst out laughing till the tears rolled down their cheeks

You're too small, David, far too small!

For a mouse to fight a giant, well, it's simply farcical.

You know you wouldn't stand a chance,

He'd cut you up and send you back before you could advance.

You're too small, David, far too small!

You're too small, David, far too small!

For a boy to fight Goliath, well, it's simply laughable.

You know you only can be crushed,

He'd tramp you under foot and grind you down into the dust.

You're too small, David, far too small.

But, since there's no one else instead,

You'd better put on armour and a helmet on your head.

But David trusted in the Lord.

He wouldn't put on armour and he wouldn't take a sword.

He only took his staff and sling

And picked up five small pebbles from a nearby spring.

He slowly walked out all alone –

The youngest son of Jesse armed with only a stone.

Goliath cried –
Do you think I lied,
Don't you take me seriously?
Goliath bellowed –
Are you so yellow
You daren't face your enemy?
Goliath cursed –
I'll do my worst
Against this mockery!
Goliath roared –
A boy with no sword
Won't get the better of me!

But the Lord was with David, and the Lord was bound to win
And He guided the stone as the stone left the sling
So it struck Goliath's forehead and it sank right in.

Goliath fell forward, yes, Goliath was dead,
So David took a sword and he cut off his head.
The Philistines panicked and they turned and fled.

It just goes to show what this tale can tell -
That even the weakest can excel.
The Lord said, Good, David, you've done well.